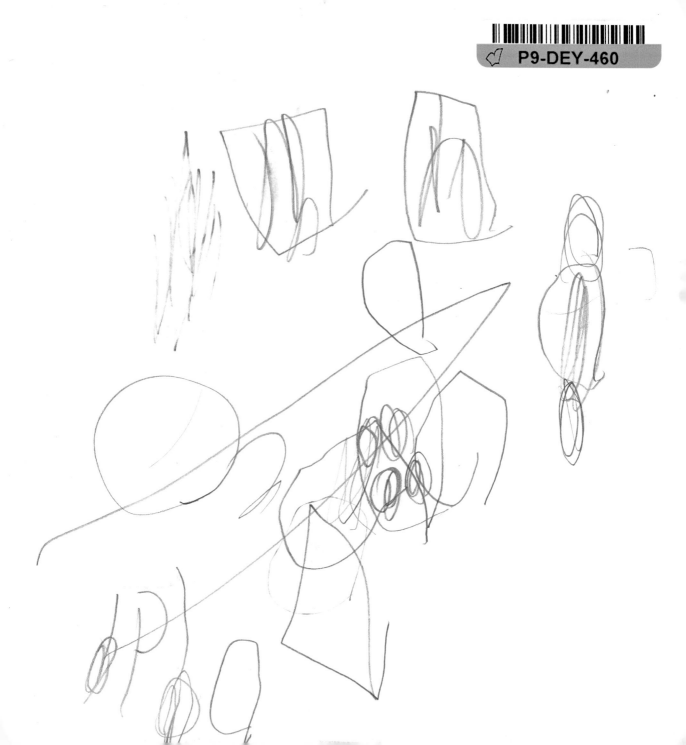

Cool PIZZA
to make & bake

Easy Recipes for Kids to Cook

Lisa Wagner

ABDO
Publishing Company

TO ADULT HELPERS

You're invited to assist an up-and-coming chef in a kitchen near you! And it will pay off in many ways. Your children can develop new skills, gain confidence, and make some delicious food while learning to cook. What's more, it's going to be a lot of fun!

These recipes are designed to let children cook independently as much as possible. Encourage them to do whatever they are able to do on their own. Also encourage them to try the variations supplied with each recipe and to experiment with their own ideas. Building creativity into the cooking process encourages children to think like real chefs.

Before getting started, set some ground rules about using the kitchen, cooking tools, and ingredients. Most important, adult supervision is a must whenever a child uses the stove, oven, or sharp tools. (Look for the Hot Stuff! and Super Sharp! symbols.)

So, put on your aprons and stand by. Let your young chefs take the lead. Watch and learn. Taste their creations. Praise their efforts. Enjoy the culinary adventure!

Visit us at www.abdopublishing.com

Published by ABDO Publishing Company, 4940 Viking Drive, Edina, Minnesota 55435. Copyright © 2007 by Abdo Consulting Group, Inc. International copyrights reserved in all countries. No part of this book may be reproduced in any form without written permission from the publisher. The Checkerboard Library™ is a trademark and logo of ABDO Publishing Company.

Printed in the United States.

Design and Production: Mighty Media, Inc.
Art Direction: Anders Hanson
Photo Credits: Anders Hanson, Shutterstock
Series Editor: Pam Price

The following manufacturers/names appearing in this book are trademarks: Pyrex®, Reynolds® Cut-Rite®, King Arthur® Flour, Bella® Olive Oil, Ziploc® Easy Zipper®, Fleischmann's® Active Dry Yeast, Morton® Iodized Salt, Muir Glen® Tomato Sauce

Library of Congress Cataloging-in-Publication Data

Wagner, Lisa, 1958-
  Cool pizza to make & bake : easy recipes for kids to cook / Lisa Wagner.
     p. cm. -- (Cool cooking)
  Includes index.
  ISBN-13: 978-1-59928-725-6
  ISBN-10: 1-59928-725-0
  1. Pizza--Juvenile literature. I. Title. II. Title: Cool pizza to make and bake.

TX770.P58W34 2007
641.8'248--dc22
                    2006032750

Table of Contents

What Makes Cooking So Cool

Welcome to the world of cooking! The cool thing about cooking is that you are the chef! You get to decide what to cook, how to cook, and what ingredients you want to use.

Everything you need to know to get started is in this book. You will learn the basic cooking terms and tools. All of the recipes in this book require only basic kitchen equipment. All the tools you will need are pictured on pages 8 through 9.

Most of the ingredients used in these recipes are shown on pages 12 through 13. This will help you identify the items for your grocery list. You want to find the freshest ingredients possible when shopping. You may notice some foods marked *organic*. This means that the food was grown using earth-friendly fertilizers and pest control methods.

This book is all about making delicious homemade pizza. It is easy to make dough and sauce from scratch. Make pizza for meals, snacks, and especially for parties! Serve pizza with a fresh green salad for a meal that is delicious and nutritious!

Most of the recipes have variations, so you can be creative. A recipe can be different every time you make it. Get inspired and give a recipe your original touch. Being a cook is like being an artist in the kitchen. The most important ingredient is imagination!

GET THE PICTURE!

When a step number in a recipe has a dotted circle around it, look for the picture that goes with it. The circle around the photo will be the same color as the step number.

The Basics

Get going in the right direction with a few important basics!

ASK PERMISSION

> Before you cook, get permission to use the kitchen, cooking tools, and ingredients.

> If you'd like to do everything by yourself, say so. As long as you can do it safely, do it.

> When you need help, ask. Always get help when you use the stove or oven.

BE PREPARED

> Being well organized is a chef's secret ingredient for success!

> Read through the entire recipe before you do anything else.

> Gather all your cooking tools and ingredients.

> Get the ingredients ready. The list of ingredients tells how to prepare each item.

> Put each prepared ingredient into a separate bowl.

> Read the recipe instructions carefully. Do the steps in the order they are listed.

BE SMART, BE SAFE

> If you use the stove or oven, you need an adult in the kitchen with you.

> Never use the stove or oven if you are home alone!

> Always get an adult to help with the hot jobs, such as draining boiling water.

> Have an adult nearby when you are using a sharp tool such as a knife, peeler, or grater. Always use sharp tools with care.

> Always turn pot handles toward the back of the stove. This helps prevent you from accidentally knocking over pots.

> Prevent accidents by working slowly and carefully. Take your time.

> If you get hurt, let an adult know right away!

BE NEAT AND CLEAN

> Start with clean hands, clean tools, and a clean work surface.

> Tie back long hair so it stays out of the way and out of the food.

> Wear comfortable clothing and roll up your sleeves.

> Aprons and chef hats are optional!

Make a Good Match!

Have fun and invent your own recipes by substituting one ingredient for another. Use the same amount of the substitute ingredient as the one it is replacing. The only thing you need to remember is to make a good match. It is best to make substitutions with dry ingredients, fruits, or vegetables. For example, if you prefer red peppers to green peppers, go ahead and use them. If a recipe calls for pepperoni, try using sausage instead.

KEY SYMBOLS

In this book, you will see some symbols beside the recipes. Here is what they mean.

HOT STUFF!

The recipe requires the use of a stove or oven. You need adult assistance and supervision.

SUPER SHARP!

A sharp tool such as a peeler, knife, or grater is needed. Get an adult to stand by.

EVEN COOLER!

This symbol means adventure! It could be a tip for making the recipe spicier. Sometimes it's a wild variation using an unusual ingredient. Give it a try! Get inspired and invent your own super-cool ideas.

MEASURING

Most ingredients are measured by the cup, tablespoon, or teaspoon.

Measuring cups and spoons come in a variety of sizes. An amount is printed or etched on each one to show how much it holds. To measure ½ cup, use the measuring cup marked ½ cup and fill it to the top.

Some measuring cups are large and have marks showing various amounts.

Ingredients such as meat and cheese are measured by weight in ounces or pounds. You purchase them by weight too.

TIP: To measure flour, spoon flour into a measuring cup. Fill the measuring cup to overflowing. Then use a table knife to scrape the excess flour back into the bag or canister.

The Tool Box

A box on the bottom of the first page of each recipe lists the tools you need. When you come across a tool you don't know, turn back to these pages.

MIXING BOWLS

CUTTING BOARD

SMALL SHARP KNIFE

PIZZA CUTTER

MEASURING CUPS

MEASURING SPOONS

GLASS MEASURING CUP

PREP BOWLS

GRATER

CAN OPENER

SPOON

FORK

TABLE KNIFE

ROUND PIZZA PAN

BAKING SHEET

PIZZA STONE

SAUCEPAN WITH COVER

PLATE

WAXED PAPER

ROLLING PIN

TOWELS

TIMER

POT HOLDER

FOOD PROCESSOR

Cool Cooking Terms

You need to learn the basic cooking terms and the actions that go with them. Whenever you need to remind yourself, just turn back to these pages.

Most ingredients need preparation before they are cooked or assembled. Look at the list of ingredients beside the recipe. After some items, you'll see words such as *chopped*, *sliced*, or *diced*. These words tell you how to prepare the ingredients.

FIRST THINGS FIRST

Always wash fruit and vegetables well. Rinse them under cold water. Pat them dry with a towel. Then they won't slip when you cut them.

PEEL

Peel means to remove the skin. To peel onion or garlic, remove the papery shell. Trim each end with a sharp knife. Then peel off the outer layer with your fingers. Never put garlic or onion peels in a food disposer!

CHOP

Chop means to cut things into small pieces. The more you chop, the smaller the pieces. If a recipe says finely chopped, it means you need very small pieces.

CUBE OR DICE

Cube and *dice* mean to cut cube or dice shapes. Usually *dice* refers to smaller pieces, and *cube* refers to larger pieces. Often a recipe will give you a dimension, such as ¼-inch dice.

TIP: Use two steps to dice or cube. First make all your cuts going one direction. Then turn the cutting board and make the crosscuts.

SLICE

Slice means to cut food into pieces of the same thickness.

MINCE

Mince means to cut the food into the tiniest possible pieces. Garlic is often minced and sometimes onion is too.

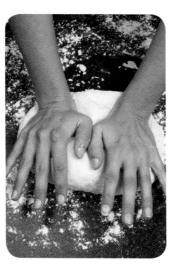

KNEAD

Knead means to use your hands to make dough smooth. Fold the dough in half and press down on it. Turn the dough sideways, fold it in half again, and press down on it again. Continue to turn, fold, and press the dough until it is smooth and stretchy.

GRATE

Grate means to shred something into small pieces using a grater. A grater has surfaces covered in holes with raised, sharp edges. You rub the food against a surface using firm pressure.

MIX

When you mix, you stir ingredients together, usually with a large spoon. *Blend* is another word for *mix*.

The Coolest Ingredients

ALL-PURPOSE
WHITE FLOUR

PITA BREAD

BAGEL

ACTIVE DRY YEAST

MONTEREY JACK CHEESE

MOZZARELLA CHEESE

PARMESAN CHEESE

CHEDDAR CHEESE

MUSHROOMS

BLACK OLIVES

SUGAR

PEPPERONI

CANADIAN BACON

PINEAPPLE, FRESH
OR CANNED

Get Fresh!

Dried herbs are stronger than fresh herbs. If you substitute fresh herbs for dried herbs, use at least three times as much as the recipe calls for. For example, if the recipe says 1 teaspoon dried basil, use 3 teaspoons chopped fresh basil.

SCALLIONS

ONION

PINE NUTS

GREEN PEPPER

OLIVE OIL

SALT

GARLIC

CANNED TOMATO PASTE

CHUNKY TOMATO SAUCE

FRESH BASIL

BUTTER

DRIED OREGANO

DRIED BASIL

GROUND BLACK PEPPER

Pizza Basics

Here are a few tips to help
you make pizza like a pro!

PIZZA ON A STONE

Some chefs like to use a pizza stone. This is a special **ceramic** disk that can get very hot without breaking. The stone goes in the oven before the heat is turned on. As the oven heats, so does the stone. Baking pizza on a stone makes a wonderful crust. If you have a pizza stone, try it!

Prepare your pizza on a lightly floured baking sheet without raised edges. When the pizza is topped, have your adult helper slide it onto the hot stone.

Hot, Hot, Hot!

You have to bake pizza in a very hot oven. The crust needs high heat to become crisp and golden brown. Always preheat your oven for at least a half hour before you bake pizza. And always have your adult helper move the pizza in and out of the oven.

EASY DOES IT

Lightly oil the pizza pan or baking sheet. You need only ½ teaspoon of olive oil to coat a pizza pan. Use waxed paper to spread the olive oil over the pan.

Topping the pizza with tasty ingredients is your chance to really get creative. But for the perfect pizza, take it easy! A thin layer of sauce is all you need. Too much sauce makes a soggy pizza crust.

YES

NO

YES

NO

Spread toppings evenly over the pizza and don't overdo it. The crust won't bake as fast as the rest of the pizza if there are too many toppings. This tip doesn't apply to the cheese though. You can always add more cheese if you like an extra-cheesy pizza!

Perfect Pizza Dough

Now your kitchen will be the
best pizza place in town!

MAKES 4 10-INCH PIZZA CRUSTS

1²/₃ cups warm water
(110 degrees)

1 packet active dry yeast

4 cups all-purpose flour,
plus extra for the work
surface

1 teaspoon salt

1 tablespoon olive oil

TOOLS:

Glass measuring cup	Mixing bowl
Measuring cups	Fork
Measuring spoons	Table knife
Prep bowls	Rolling pin

1 Pour the water into a glass measuring cup and add the yeast. Let it stand until the yeast dissolves and the mixture **froths**, about 5 minutes.

2 Mix the flour and salt in a large mixing bowl.

3 Add the olive oil to the yeast mixture.

4 Slowly pour the yeast mixture into the flour and stir with a fork. When it gets hard to stir with the fork, use your hands.

5 Squish the dough around to combine all the ingredients.

6 Try to form the dough into a ball. When it holds together in a ball shape, it is ready to knead.

TIP: Test the water temperature by sprinkling a few drops on the inside of your wrist. The water should feel a little warmer than your skin, but not much warmer. If the water is too warm, it will kill the yeast and keep it from frothing.

NOTE: Before you begin, wash your hands very well! You will use your hands to mix and knead the dough.

7 Sprinkle some flour on a work surface, such as a clean table, cutting board, or countertop. Use only enough flour to keep the dough from sticking to the surface.

8 Knead the dough on the floured work surface for about 5 minutes. It will feel smooth and stretchy when it is ready to use.

9 Make the dough into a ball and flatten it slightly. Then cut it into four equal pieces.

10 Use your hands to shape each piece of dough into a smooth ball.

11 Put one of the balls on the floured surface and roll it out with a rolling pin until it is between ⅛-inch and ¼-inch thick. Now you're almost ready to top that pizza crust! Make the Pizza-Riffic Sauce (page 20). Then follow the baking instructions in the Best-Ever Pizza recipe (page 22).

> **TIP:** If you don't have a rolling pin, you can still make a perfect pizza. Just flatten the small ball of dough on the floured surface. Then push, pull, pat, and stretch it until you have a circle.

TIP: If you can't use all your dough at once, freeze it. Put the dough in a plastic bag, squeeze out the air, and seal the bag. Frozen pizza dough will keep for about 3 months. Before you use it, let the dough thaw for about 2 hours at room temperature. Knead it briefly between your hands before you roll it out.

TIP: To make two large pizzas, cut the dough into two pieces instead of four. You can use a baking sheet and make a rectangular pizza. In Italy, many of the pizzas are rectangular!

Even Cooler!

Form the pizza dough into an unusual shape. Make a heart-shaped pizza for Valentine's Day. Try a football-shaped pizza for a Super Bowl party. Use your imagination and have fun!

Pizza-Riffic Sauce

A great crust deserves a great sauce. Try this one!

MAKES 2 CUPS OF SAUCE

INGREDIENTS

2 tablespoons olive oil
2 garlic cloves, minced
¼ cup minced onion
2 tablespoons tomato paste
1 14½-ounce can chunky tomato sauce
¼ cup water
1 teaspoon dried oregano
1 teaspoon dried basil
½ teaspoon sugar
1 teaspoon salt
¼ teaspoon pepper

TOOLS:
Saucepan
Cutting board
Small sharp knife

Measuring cups
Measuring spoons
Can opener

Prep bowls
Wooden spoon

1 Heat the olive oil in a saucepan.

2 Add the garlic and onion and cook over low heat. Stir often and cook until the onion is almost transparent. Keep the heat low so the garlic doesn't brown.

3 Add the tomato paste and stir until it is blended in.

4 Add the tomato sauce, water, herbs, sugar, salt, and pepper. Bring the mixture to a boil over medium heat, stirring often.

5 Turn down the heat and let the mixture cook over low heat for 5 minutes. The sauce will get thicker as it cooks.

Important!

Thick sauces such as this one can erupt and spray hot droplets of sauce in the air. Stir the sauce often to prevent steam buildup and eruptions.

Variations

> Want the sauce to be even thicker? Stir in an additional tablespoon of tomato paste and cook the sauce 5 minutes longer.

> Use fresh herbs instead of dried herbs.

Even Cooler!

Make the sauce with fresh tomatoes. Instead of a can of tomato sauce, use 2 large, very ripe tomatoes. Dice the tomatoes into ¼-inch pieces using a **serrated** knife. To thicken the sauce, increase the cooking time to 10 minutes.

Best-Ever Pizza

Your local pizza parlor will want this recipe!

MAKES 2
10-INCH PIZZAS

TOOLS: Grater
Measuring cups
Measuring spoons
Prep bowls

Baking sheet or pizza pans
Waxed paper
Spoon
Pizza cutter

1 Preheat the oven to 450 degrees.

2 Use waxed paper to lightly coat each pan with ½ teaspoon of olive oil.

3 Divide the pizza dough into two balls. Roll out the dough according to the instructions on page 18. Put the rolled-out dough on the pizza pans.

4 Use ½ cup of Pizza-Riffic Sauce for each pizza. Spread the sauce over the dough to within 1 inch of the edge. Use the back of a spoon to spread the sauce evenly.

5 Sprinkle the mozzarella cheese evenly over the sauce. Use half the cheese for each pizza. Then do the same with the other cheeses.

TIP: To bake two pizzas at the same time, put one on the lowest rack. Put the other on the next rack up. Halfway through the baking time, switch the positions of the pans.

There are many delicious ingredients you can use to top a pizza. Make your own creative combinations by choosing ingredients from this list.

> Sliced pepperoni
> Cooked Italian sausage
> Canadian bacon
> Diced chicken
> Anchovies
> Green or red pepper
> Jalapeño pepper
> Red onion

> Scallion
> Pineapple
> Spinach
> Ham
> Fresh tomato
> Broccoli
> Mushroom
> Olives

6 When the oven is hot, have your adult helper put the pizza in the oven. Use the lowest rack in the oven.

7 Bake for 10 to 12 minutes, or until the cheese is bubbling.

8 Have your adult helper remove the pizza from the oven.

9 Let the pizza stand for 10 minutes. Then cut it with a pizza cutter or a knife and serve it!

Variations

> This recipe can make one large, rectangular pizza instead of two small, round pizzas. Just roll the dough into a rectangular shape before you put it on a baking sheet. Follow the instructions beginning with Step 4 above, using all the sauce and all the cheese.

Even Cooler!

For a spicy pizza, skip the Cheddar and Monterey Jack cheeses. Instead, use 2 cups of grated mozzarella cheese, 1½ cups of pepper jack cheese, and ½ cup of Parmesan cheese.

INGREDIENTS

½ recipe Perfect Pizza Dough (page 16)
1 cup Pizza-Riffic Sauce (page 20)
1 teaspoon olive oil

FOR PEPPERONI LOVER'S COMBO

28 slices pepperoni
½ cup chopped onion
2½ cups grated mozzarella cheese

FOR HAWAIIAN PIZZA

8 ounces Canadian bacon,
   cut into ½-inch cubes
1½ cups cubed pineapple
1 green pepper, sliced in rings
2½ cups grated mozzarella cheese

Coolest Combo Pizza

Just a couple of ideas to get your imagination going!

EACH COMBO MAKES 2
10-INCH PIZZAS

1 Follow steps 1 through 4 on page 23.

2 Spread the cheese evenly over the pizza sauce. Then add the meat and veggies. Use half of the total amount of each ingredient for each pizza.

3 Continue with steps 6 through 9 on page 24.

TOOLS:
Grater
Measuring cups
Measuring spoons
Cutting board

Small sharp knife
Prep bowls
Baking sheet
   or pizza pans

Waxed paper
Spoon
Pizza cutter

Pita Pizza

Pita bread makes a really terrific pizza crust!

MAKES 4 PIZZAS

INGREDIENTS

4 white or whole wheat pita rounds

1 cup Pizza-Riffic Sauce (page 20)

2 cups grated mozzarella cheese

TOOLS: Grater   Spoon
Measuring cups   Pizza cutter
Baking sheet

1 Preheat the oven to 425 degrees.

2 Place the pita rounds on a baking sheet. Put ¼ cup of sauce on each pita and spread it evenly with the back of a spoon.

3 Sprinkle ½ cup of cheese on each pita round.

4 Bake for 7 to 8 minutes, or until the cheese is bubbly. Have your adult helper remove the pizzas from the oven.

5 Let the pizzas stand for 5 minutes. Cut them into wedges with a pizza cutter or a knife and serve them!

Variations

> Add a few slices of pepperoni or Canadian bacon. Or, add veggies such as black or green olives, fresh mushrooms, green or red pepper, onion, or broccoli. For best results, use about 1/3 cup of mixed ingredients for each pizza.

Bagel Veggie Pizza

Mini pizzas that make a meal!

MAKES 8 PIZZAS

INGREDIENTS

4 bagels, split in half
8 tablespoons Pizza-Riffic Sauce (page 20)
½ cup sliced black olives
8 mushrooms, thinly sliced
2 scallions, chopped
2 cups grated mozzarella cheese

TOOLS:
Cutting board
Small sharp knife
Grater
Measuring cup
Measuring spoons
Baking sheet
Spoon

1 Preheat the oven to 400 degrees.

2 Place the bagel halves on a baking sheet with the cut side facing up. Put 1 tablespoon of sauce on each bagel half and spread it evenly with the back of a spoon.

3 Divide the veggies evenly among the bagel halves.

4 Top each bagel half with ¼ cup of cheese.

5 Bake for 8 to 10 minutes, or until the cheese is bubbly.

6 Let the pizzas stand for five minutes after your adult helper removes them from the oven.

Variations

> Make pepperoni bagel pizzas by putting 4 to 6 slices of pepperoni on each bagel half.

> Create your own original bagel pizzas. Try other toppings such as broccoli, chopped green or red peppers, or diced onion.

> Experiment with different types of cheese, such as Cheddar or Monterey Jack.

Presto Pesto!

Use pesto in place of pizza sauce for an excellent veggie pizza!

MAKES 1½ CUPS

INGREDIENTS

3 cups loosely packed fresh basil leaves

2 tablespoons butter

2 cloves garlic, minced

¾ cup grated Parmesan cheese

¼ cup pine nuts, optional

1 teaspoon salt

Fresh ground pepper, optional

½ cup olive oil

1 Have an adult help you assemble the **food processor**. Then put all the ingredients except the olive oil in the work bowl of the food processor.

2 Coarsely chop the ingredients by using the pulse button or by quickly turning the machine on and off. In other words, don't just turn on the food processor and let it grind everything to a paste. You should see rough particles of all the ingredients.

3 With the motor running, add the olive oil through the open tube at the top. Now the mixture should look like a paste. If it is too dry, add more olive oil.

4 Use ¾ cup of pesto for each 10-inch pizza. Top with veggies and cheese and bake as directed on page 24.

TOOLS: Measuring cups Small sharp knife
Measuring spoons Grater
Prep bowls Food processor

Glossary

ceramic – of or relating to a nonmetallic product, such as pottery or porcelain.

food processor – a kitchen appliance with blades that can slice, shred, and blend food.

froth – to cause the surface of a liquid to become covered with bubbles.

serrated – having a jagged edge.

Web Sites

To learn more about cool cooking, visit ABDO Publishing Company on the World Wide Web at **www.abdopublishing.com**. Web sites about cool cooking are featured on our Book Links page. These links are routinely monitored and updated to provide the most current information available.

Index